Table of Contents

Introduction.. 3
Chapter 1: Introduction to Digital Marketing Agencies.. 5
Chapter 2: Defining Your Agency's Niche and Unique Value Proposition................................... 12
Chapter 3: Setting Up Your Digital Marketing Agency.. 16
Chapter 4: Building Your Agency's Brand and Online Presence... 20
Chapter 5: Acquiring Clients and Generating Leads... 24
Chapter 6: Providing Exceptional Client Service and Delivering Results..................................... 29
Chapter 7: Scaling Your Agency and Growing Your Team.. 33
Chapter 8: Diversifying Your Agency's Services and Revenue Streams..................................... 40
Chapter 9: Managing Finances, Budgets, and Profitability.. 44
Chapter 10: Continuously Innovating and Adapting in the Digital Marketing Landscape.. 49

Introduction

Hello and welcome to "The Ultimate Guide on How to Start a Digital Marketing Agency." If you're here, you're probably excited about the idea of diving into the world of digital marketing, and you're in the right place. This book is packed with valuable insights and practical tips that will help you establish and run a successful digital marketing agency.

Let's face it, the digital landscape has completely transformed the way businesses operate and market their products and services. More than ever, businesses are recognizing the importance of having a strong online presence. This has led to an explosion in the demand for digital marketing agencies. For aspiring entrepreneurs like you, this is a golden opportunity to step into a booming industry.

In this guide, we're going to cover a lot of ground. We'll explore the ins and outs of starting and growing your digital marketing agency. It doesn't matter if you have a background in marketing or if you're completely new to the field; this book is designed to give you the knowledge and tools you need to build a thriving agency from the ground up.

We'll start with the basics, helping you understand what digital marketing is all about and why it's so crucial in today's business world. Then, we'll move on to the practical steps you'll need to take to get your agency off the ground. From setting up your business, finding your niche, and building a team, to creating effective marketing strategies for your clients, we've got you covered.

But we won't stop there. Running a successful digital marketing agency involves more than just knowing the right tactics. We'll also delve into how to manage your agency, how to keep your clients happy, and how to keep up with the ever-changing digital landscape.

By the end of this book, you'll have a comprehensive understanding of what it takes to start and run a digital marketing agency. You'll be equipped with practical knowledge and strategies that you can apply to your own business. So, get ready to embark on this exciting journey. Your dream of running a successful digital marketing agency is within reach, and we're here to help you every step of the way.

Chapter 1: Introduction to Digital Marketing Agencies

Welcome to the fascinating world of digital marketing agencies! In this first chapter, we'll dive deep into the pivotal role and significance of these agencies in today's fast-paced business environment. We'll explore the myriad services they offer, such as search engine optimization (SEO), pay-per-click (PPC) advertising, social media marketing, content marketing, and so much more. By understanding these services, you'll be better equipped to define the scope and direction of your agency.

But that's not all. We'll also discuss the crucial process of setting clear goals and objectives for your digital marketing agency. It's essential to have a well-defined vision and mission to steer your strategic decisions and ensure long-term success. Let's get started on this exciting journey!

Defining Your Agency's Niche and Unique Value Proposition

In Chapter 2, we shift our focus to carving out your agency's niche and crafting a unique value proposition. By honing in on a specific market segment or industry, you can position your agency as a go-to expert in that field. We'll walk you through strategies for researching target clients, analyzing competitors, and staying on top of market trends to spot opportunities for differentiation.

Crafting a compelling unique value proposition is vital in a crowded market. We'll guide you through the process of highlighting your agency's expertise, experience, and unique selling points, ensuring you attract and retain clients effectively. Ready to stand out from the competition? Let's dive in!

Setting Up Your Digital Marketing Agency

Chapter 3 is all about laying the groundwork for your digital marketing agency from a structural and operational perspective. We'll discuss critical considerations like choosing the right business structure, selecting a fitting name, and establishing the legal entity for your agency. Additionally, we'll guide you through the steps of registering your agency with relevant authorities and obtaining necessary licenses and permits.

Setting up essential business operations, including office space, equipment, software, and team structure, will also be covered. By the end of this chapter, you'll have a solid foundation to build upon. Let's get your agency up and running!

Building Your Agency's Brand and Online Presence

In the digital marketing industry, a strong brand and online presence are crucial for attracting clients and establishing credibility. In Chapter 4, we'll delve into the importance of developing a professional brand identity, complete with a logo and visual assets that reflect your agency's values and expertise.

Creating a professional website that showcases your agency's services, portfolio, case studies, and client testimonials will be a focal point. We'll also explore the significance of establishing a presence on various social media platforms and professional networking sites to expand your reach and attract potential leads. Ready to make a lasting impression? Let's get started!

Acquiring Clients and Generating Leads

Now that your agency is set up, it's time to focus on acquiring clients and generating leads. In Chapter 5, we'll delve into strategies and tactics to attract potential clients effectively. Developing a comprehensive marketing strategy and plan is essential for this purpose.

We'll explore various lead generation tactics, such as content marketing, email marketing, networking, and outreach. Leveraging your network, referrals, and partnerships will also play a crucial role in generating initial leads and securing your first clients. Ready to grow your client base? Let's dive in!

Providing Exceptional Client Service and Delivering Results

Client satisfaction and delivering tangible results are paramount for the long-term success of your digital marketing agency. In Chapter 6, we'll focus on understanding client needs, goals, and expectations for digital marketing services.

We'll guide you through the process of developing customized strategies, campaigns, and solutions to meet client objectives and deliver measurable results. Effective communication, regular updates, transparent reporting, and constructive feedback will be explored to foster strong client relationships and ensure client satisfaction. Let's ensure your clients are happy and your results are impressive!

Scaling Your Agency and Growing Your Team

As your digital marketing agency begins to thrive, scaling and growing your team becomes a priority. In Chapter 7, we'll provide insights on expanding your agency's capabilities by hiring and onboarding talented professionals with expertise in various digital marketing disciplines.

Establishing processes, systems, and workflows to streamline operations and accommodate higher client loads will be crucial for scalability. We'll also explore the importance of developing a collaborative culture that fosters innovation and continuous learning among your team members. Ready to take your agency to the next level? Let's get started!

Diversifying Your Agency's Services and Revenue Streams

In Chapter 8, we'll focus on expanding your agency's services and revenue streams. As the digital marketing landscape evolves, it's essential to adapt and diversify your offerings to meet changing client needs and market demands.

We'll explore additional revenue streams such as consulting, training, workshops, or white-label services. Developing strategic partnerships and collaborations will also be discussed as a means to enhance your agency's capabilities and expand your client base. Ready to diversify and grow? Let's dive in!

Managing Finances, Budgets, and Profitability

Managing finances, budgets, and profitability is a critical aspect of running a successful digital marketing agency. In Chapter 9, we'll discuss setting financial goals, creating budgets for your agency's operations and growth initiatives, and making informed decisions about pricing, billing, and resource allocation.

Implementing effective financial management systems and processes to track expenses, revenue, profitability, and cash flow will be explored as essential practices for long-term sustainability. Ready to master your finances? Let's get started!

Continuously Innovating and Adapting in the Digital Marketing Landscape

In the ever-changing digital marketing landscape, continuous innovation and adaptation are key. Chapter 10 emphasizes the importance of staying informed about industry trends, emerging technologies, and best practices to stay ahead of the curve.

We'll guide you on investing in ongoing education, training, and professional development for yourself and your team to ensure you consistently deliver exceptional value to your clients. Additionally, we'll explore strategies for innovating and adapting your agency's strategies, services, and offerings to meet evolving client needs and expectations.

By the end of this book, you'll be equipped with the knowledge, skills, and strategies to start, scale, and succeed in your own digital marketing agency. Let's embark on this exciting journey together and get ready to make your mark in the digital marketing industry!

Chapter 2: Defining Your Agency's Niche and Unique Value Proposition

In the bustling world of digital marketing, standing out from the crowd is no easy feat. The key to success lies in defining your agency's niche market and crafting a unique value proposition (UVP). This chapter is your roadmap to discovering your agency's specialty, understanding your target clients and competitors, and creating a compelling value proposition that makes your agency the go-to choice in your market.

Identifying Your Agency's Niche Market

To carve out a space for your agency in the competitive digital marketing landscape, it's crucial to identify a niche market or industry focus. By honing in on a specific target market, you can customize your services to address the unique needs and challenges of that sector. This specialization makes your agency more appealing to potential clients looking for expertise tailored to their industry.

Steps to Identify Your Niche Market:

1. **Evaluate Your Expertise and Passions:** Begin by assessing your

own skills, expertise, and interests. Which industries do you have experience in? What are you passionate about? Finding areas where you possess a competitive edge and genuine interest will help you shine in the marketplace.

2. **Research Market Demand:** Dive into market research to gauge the demand for digital marketing services across various industries. Look for sectors experiencing growth where there is a need for specialized digital marketing expertise. A market with high demand and limited competition can offer lucrative opportunities for your agency.

3. **Analyze Competitors:** Study your competitors to identify gaps in the market. Look for areas where they might be underserving clients or where their expertise is lacking. This will help you position your agency as a standout alternative, showcasing your unique strengths.

Researching Target Clients and Competitors

Once you've pinpointed your niche market, the next step is to research your target clients and competitors. This research will give you invaluable insights into the needs, preferences, and pain points of your audience. It will also help you understand the competitive landscape and uncover opportunities for differentiation.

Steps to Research Target Clients and Competitors:

1. **Define Your Target Audience:** Determine who your ideal clients are within your niche market. This could include specific demographics, industries, or business sizes. Understanding your target audience will enable you to tailor your marketing efforts and services to meet their specific needs.
2. **Study Competitor Strategies:** Analyze your competitors' marketing strategies, service offerings, and pricing models. Identify their strengths, weaknesses, and unique selling points. This analysis will help you find gaps in the market and position your agency as a compelling choice.
3. **Conduct Client Surveys or Interviews:** Reach out to potential clients within your target market to gather feedback and insights. Learn about their pain points, challenges, and what they look for in a digital marketing agency. This information will help you tailor your services and value proposition to address their specific needs.

Crafting a Unique Value Proposition

A unique value proposition (UVP) is a clear and concise statement that communicates the unique benefits and value your agency brings to clients. It should highlight your expertise, experience, and unique selling points that set your agency apart from competitors. Crafting a strong UVP is crucial for attracting and retaining clients.

Steps to Craft Your Unique Value Proposition:

1. **Identify Your Agency's Strengths:** Reflect on your agency's strengths, expertise, and unique capabilities. What sets your agency apart from others in the market? What value can you provide that competitors cannot? This could be specialized industry knowledge, proprietary tools or technologies, or a track record of delivering exceptional results.
2. **Understand Client Pain Points:** Consider the challenges and pain points that your target clients are facing. How can your agency address these pain points and provide a solution? Your UVP should clearly articulate the benefits that clients can expect when they choose your agency.

3. **Differentiate from Competitors:** Identify the unique selling points that set your agency apart from competitors. This could be a specialized service offering, a proprietary methodology, or a personalized approach to client relationships. Clearly communicate these differentiators in your UVP to showcase your agency's unique value.

By defining your agency's niche market and crafting a compelling unique value proposition, you will position your agency as a specialized expert capable of providing exceptional value to your target clients. This strategic approach will help you attract clients, stand out from the competition, and ultimately thrive in the dynamic digital marketing industry.

Chapter 3: Setting Up Your Digital Marketing Agency

Starting a digital marketing agency is an exciting venture, but it requires careful planning and organization to set yourself up for success. In this chapter, we'll walk you through the essential steps to get your agency off the ground. From choosing the right business structure and name to setting up your operations, we'll cover everything you need to build a solid foundation for your agency's growth.

Choosing a Business Structure, Name, and Legal Entity

The first big decision you'll need to make when starting your digital marketing agency is choosing its legal structure. The most common options are sole proprietorship, partnership, limited liability company (LLC), and corporation. Each structure has its own advantages and disadvantages, so it's wise to consult with a legal professional or an accountant to help you select the one that best aligns with your long-term goals and offers the necessary liability protection.

Once you've decided on the legal structure, it's time to pick a name for your agency. Your agency's name should reflect your brand, resonate with your target audience, and be memorable. Make sure to check that the name isn't already trademarked or in use by another business in the same industry to avoid any legal issues down the road. After settling on a name, you'll need to register it with the appropriate authorities, which varies depending on your country or state regulations. This step not only provides legal protection but also legitimizes your business, allowing you to operate officially.

Obtaining Necessary Licenses and Permits

Before you can start offering your digital marketing services to clients, you may need to secure certain licenses or permits. The specific requirements can vary based on your location and the services you plan to offer. It's crucial to research and comply with all legal obligations to avoid potential fines or other legal repercussions. Reach out to your local government agencies or consult with an attorney to determine the exact licenses and permits required for your digital marketing agency. Examples might include a general business license, professional licenses, sales tax permits, and permits related to data privacy regulations.

Setting Up Essential Business Operations

To run your digital marketing agency effectively, you'll need to establish essential business operations. This involves setting up an office space, acquiring necessary equipment and software, and defining your team structure.

When it comes to choosing an office space, consider your budget, location, and the needs of your team. Depending on the size of your agency and its remote work capabilities, you might opt for a traditional office space or a virtual office setup. The space you choose should promote productivity and foster a positive work environment.

Investing in the right equipment and software is vital for the smooth operation of your agency. You'll need items like computers, laptops, high-speed internet, project management tools, design software, and analytics platforms. Carefully assess your agency's needs and budget to determine the essential tools and technologies required to deliver top-notch services to your clients.

Lastly, think about the team structure and roles necessary to provide your services effectively. Identify the expertise needed in areas such as SEO, PPC, social media marketing, content creation, and analytics. Decide whether you'll hire in-house employees or collaborate with freelancers and contractors. Clearly define roles and responsibilities within your team to ensure smooth operations and high client satisfaction.

By meticulously setting up your agency's business structure, obtaining the necessary licenses, and establishing essential operations, you'll be well-prepared to offer exceptional digital marketing services to your clients. In the next chapter, we'll delve into the importance of building your agency's brand and establishing a strong online presence.

Chapter 4: Building Your Agency's Brand and Online Presence

Creating a strong brand and a solid online presence is essential for your digital marketing agency's success. In this chapter, we'll dive into the strategies and tactics you need to develop a professional brand identity, create an engaging website, and establish a presence on social media and professional networking platforms.

Developing a Professional Brand Identity

To stand out from competitors and attract clients, you need a professional brand identity. This includes a logo and visual assets that reflect your agency's personality and values. Let's break down the key steps to achieving this:

1. Understand Your Target Market
Before diving into design, you need to clearly understand your target market. Conduct market research to gather insights into their demographics, psychographics, and design preferences. Knowing what your audience likes and responds to will guide your branding decisions.

2. Define Your Unique Brand Personality

Your brand should have a distinct personality that resonates with your target audience. Decide if you want your brand to come across as professional, innovative, friendly, or authoritative. This decision will influence your design process and how you communicate with your audience.

3. Design a Logo
Your logo is the visual cornerstone of your brand. It should be simple, memorable, and reflective of your agency's values and services. Consider hiring a professional graphic designer to create a high-quality logo that aligns with your brand identity.

4. Create Visual Assets
Beyond your logo, you'll need to develop visual assets like brand colors, typography, and imagery. These elements should be used consistently across all marketing materials, including your website and social media profiles, to create a cohesive brand image.

Creating a Professional Website

A professional website is vital for showcasing your agency's services, portfolio, case studies, and client testimonials. It serves as the central hub where potential clients can learn about your agency and contact you. Here's how to create an effective website:

1. Define Your Website's Structure
Plan out the pages you want on your website, such as a homepage, services page, portfolio page, about us page, and contact page. Think about the needs of your target audience and how they will navigate your site.

2. Craft Compelling Content
Write clear and concise content that describes your agency's services, highlights your expertise, and addresses potential client pain points. Use a persuasive tone and incorporate keywords relevant to your industry to improve your search engine optimization (SEO).

3. Showcase Your Portfolio and Case Studies
Display your past work, success stories, and case studies to build credibility and demonstrate your expertise. Include details about the challenges you solved, the strategies you implemented, and the results you achieved.

4. Incorporate Client Testimonials
Feature testimonials from satisfied clients to build trust and credibility. Use their full name, job title, and company name to add authenticity to the testimonials.

5. Optimize for Mobile Devices
Ensure your website is mobile-responsive. With the increasing use of mobile devices, your site must adjust automatically to different

screen sizes and provide a seamless user experience across all devices.

Establishing a Presence on Social Media Platforms and Professional Networking Sites

Social media and professional networking sites are great for attracting leads, building credibility, and engaging with your target audience. Here's how to establish a strong online presence:

1. Identify the Right Platforms
Research the social media platforms and professional networking sites most relevant to your target audience. Consider factors like demographics, industry trends, and user engagement.

2. Develop a Posting Strategy
Create a content calendar and develop a strategy for consistent and engaging social media posts. Share industry news, helpful tips, case studies, and other valuable content to position your agency as a thought leader.

3. Engage with Your Audience
Respond to comments, messages, and inquiries promptly to show you value your audience's engagement. Encourage dialogue, ask questions, and participate in industry discussions to build meaningful connections.

4. Leverage Paid Advertising
Consider investing in paid social media advertising to expand your reach and target specific audience segments. Platforms like Facebook and LinkedIn offer sophisticated targeting options to help you reach your ideal clients.

By focusing on building a professional brand identity, creating a compelling website, and establishing a presence on social media and professional networking sites, you can enhance your agency's visibility, attract leads, and build credibility in the digital marketing industry.

In the next chapter, we'll dive into strategies for acquiring clients and generating leads for your digital marketing agency.

Chapter 5: Acquiring Clients and Generating Leads

Attracting and acquiring clients is a crucial aspect of running a successful digital marketing agency. In this chapter, we'll delve into the strategies and tactics you can implement to generate leads and grow your client base.

Developing a Marketing Strategy and Plan

Before diving into lead generation tactics, it's essential to develop a clear marketing strategy and plan. This will ensure that your efforts are focused and aligned with your agency's goals and objectives. Here are some steps to consider when creating your marketing strategy:

1. **Identify Your Target Audience:** Determine the specific industries, niches, or businesses that you want to serve. Understanding your target audience will help you tailor your marketing messages and tactics to their needs and preferences.
2. **Define Your Agency's Unique Selling Proposition (USP):** Clearly communicate what sets your agency apart from the competition. Your USP

could be based on your expertise, industry experience, unique strategies, or exceptional customer service.
3. **Set Marketing Goals:** Establish specific and measurable goals for your marketing efforts. These goals could include acquiring a certain number of clients within a specific time frame, reaching revenue targets, or increasing brand awareness.
4. **Select Marketing Channels:** Identify the most effective channels to reach your target audience. Consider utilizing a combination of digital marketing channels such as social media, search engine optimization (SEO), pay-per-click (PPC) advertising, content marketing, and email marketing.
5. **Craft Compelling Marketing Messages:** Develop persuasive and compelling messages that communicate the value and benefits your agency can provide to potential clients. Highlight your agency's expertise, case studies, and success stories to build credibility.

Implementing Lead Generation Tactics

Once you have a clear marketing strategy in place, it's time to implement lead generation tactics to attract potential clients. Here are some effective tactics you can utilize:

1. **Content Marketing:** Create valuable and informative content that addresses the pain points and challenges of your target audience. This content could take the form of blog posts, articles, eBooks, videos, or webinars. Share this content on your website, social media platforms, and through email newsletters to attract potential clients and establish your agency as an industry thought leader.
2. **Email Marketing:** Build an email list of potential clients who have shown interest in your agency's services. Utilize email marketing campaigns to nurture leads and provide valuable information to your subscribers. Offer exclusive content, special promotions, or personalized consultations to encourage potential clients to engage with your agency.
3. **Networking and Outreach:** Attend industry conferences, events, and meetups to connect with potential clients and build relationships. Engage in online forums and communities where your target audience is active. Proactively reach out to individuals and businesses that align with your agency's niche to explore partnership or collaboration opportunities.
4. **Referrals and Testimonials:** Encourage your existing clients to refer your agency to their network. Offer

incentives or rewards for referrals. Additionally, collect testimonials from satisfied clients and showcase them on your website and social media platforms. Positive testimonials can significantly boost your agency's credibility and attract new clients.

Leveraging Your Network, Referrals, and Partnerships

In addition to the lead generation tactics mentioned above, it's important to leverage your existing network, referrals, and partnerships to generate initial leads and clients for your agency. Here are some strategies to consider:

1. **Tap into Your Personal and Professional Network:** Reach out to friends, family, former colleagues, and acquaintances who may be in need of digital marketing services. Let them know about your agency and the value you can provide.
2. **Ask for Referrals:** Don't be afraid to ask your satisfied clients for referrals. Offer incentives for successful referrals to encourage your clients to refer your agency to their connections.
3. **Develop Strategic Partnerships:** Identify complementary businesses or

service providers that target the same audience as your agency. Explore partnership opportunities where you can refer clients to each other, collaborate on joint marketing campaigns, or offer bundled services.

By implementing these lead generation tactics and leveraging your network, referrals, and partnerships, you can generate initial leads and clients for your digital marketing agency. Consistency, persistence, and a commitment to delivering exceptional service will help you build a strong client base and grow your business.

Chapter 6: Providing Exceptional Client Service and Delivering Results

Understanding Client Needs, Goals, and Expectations

In the world of digital marketing, offering exceptional client service and delivering results hinges on a profound understanding of your clients' needs, goals, and expectations. Each client is unique, with distinct objectives they aim to achieve through digital marketing. This means a one-size-fits-all approach simply won't cut it.

To get started, it's essential to have open and transparent conversations with your clients. Dive deep into understanding their business, target audience, and overall marketing objectives. Ask plenty of questions and, just as importantly, listen actively to their responses. This dialogue helps uncover their pain points, challenges, and expectations, which is crucial for crafting comprehensive and effective strategies.

Aligning your understanding of the clients' goals with their broader business objectives is also vital. Determine how digital marketing can play a role in their success and identify key performance indicators (KPIs) to measure the effectiveness of your efforts. With a clear grasp of what your clients aim to achieve, you can develop strategies that deliver tangible and measurable results.

Developing Customized Strategies, Campaigns, and Solutions

Once you've thoroughly understood your clients' needs and goals, the next step is to develop tailored strategies, campaigns, and solutions. Avoid the temptation to apply a generic approach. Instead, focus on customizing your services to meet each client's unique requirements.

Start by conducting thorough research and analysis. This groundwork will help you pinpoint the most effective digital marketing channels, tactics, and tools that align with your clients' goals. Consider factors like their target audience, industry trends, and competition. Based on this research, create comprehensive and actionable plans outlining the steps needed to achieve your clients' objectives. Break down these plans into specific campaigns and initiatives, each with clear goals, timelines, and deliverables. This structured approach keeps you organized and ensures consistent progress toward achieving results.

Remember, monitoring the performance of your campaigns and strategies is crucial. Use performance metrics and analytics to assess their effectiveness and make data-driven decisions. By keeping a close eye on the results and making necessary adjustments, you can optimize your strategies and campaigns to deliver the best possible outcomes for your clients.

Communicating Transparently and Providing Regular Updates

Effective communication is the cornerstone of building strong client relationships and delivering exceptional service. Maintain open lines of communication with your clients, providing regular updates and reports on the progress and results of your digital marketing efforts.

When presenting reports, ensure they are clear and concise, highlighting the key metrics and insights relevant to your clients' goals. Use visual aids like charts and graphs to make the data easy to understand. Alongside these reports, provide detailed explanations and recommendations, showcasing your expertise and insights.

Establish a regular communication schedule with your clients, including weekly or monthly check-ins, strategy sessions, or progress meetings. During these interactions, discuss campaign performance, address any concerns or questions, and present new opportunities or recommendations.

Transparency is key in client communication. Be honest about the results and challenges you are facing, and provide actionable solutions to overcome any obstacles. Create an environment of trust and collaboration where clients feel comfortable expressing their needs and expectations.

Finally, actively seek feedback from your clients. Regularly ask for their input, opinions, and suggestions. This continuous feedback loop helps you improve your services and ensures you are meeting their expectations.

By understanding client needs, developing customized strategies, and maintaining transparent communication, you can provide exceptional client service and deliver the results they are looking for. This approach not only helps in retaining existing clients but also attracts new ones through positive word-of-mouth and a strong reputation.

Chapter 7: Scaling Your Agency and Growing Your Team

Ensuring the growth and success of your digital marketing agency hinges on your ability to scale operations and expand your team effectively. In this chapter, we'll walk you through the essential steps to hiring and onboarding talented professionals, establishing efficient processes and systems, and fostering a culture of collaboration, innovation, and continuous learning within your agency.

Hiring and Onboarding Talented Professionals

As your agency grows, it's crucial to bring in skilled professionals with expertise in various digital marketing disciplines to meet the increasing demands of your clients. Here's a detailed guide on how to do it successfully:

1. **Define the Roles and Expertise Needed:**
     - Start by assessing your agency's current and future needs. Determine the specific roles and expertise required, such as SEO specialists, PPC managers, social media strategists, content creators, and project managers.

2. **Develop Job Descriptions:**
   - Craft detailed job descriptions that clearly outline responsibilities, required skills, qualifications, and expected outcomes. This will help attract candidates who are the right fit for your agency's needs.
3. **Utilize Multiple Recruitment Channels:**
   - Advertise job openings on various platforms like job boards, industry-specific websites, social media, and professional networking sites. Don't forget to leverage your existing network and ask for referrals to find potential candidates.

4. **Conduct Thorough Interviews:**
   - Screen candidates through multiple rounds of interviews to assess their skills, experience, cultural fit, and attitude. Use behavioral and situational questions to gauge their problem-solving abilities and teamwork skills.
5. **Check References and Portfolios:**
   - Before making a final decision, contact references provided by

the candidates to validate their skills and performance. Additionally, review their portfolios to assess the quality of their previous work.

6. **Onboarding and Training:**
    - Once you've selected the right candidates, create a comprehensive onboarding program to familiarize them with your agency's culture, processes, and tools. Provide training opportunities to enhance their skills and ensure they are well-equipped to meet client expectations.

Establishing Processes, Systems, and Workflows

To effectively scale your agency, you need to establish streamlined processes, systems, and workflows. These steps will improve operational efficiency and enable your team to handle a growing volume of work:

1. **Clearly Define Processes:**
    - Document and communicate standard operating procedures (SOPs) for various tasks, such as client onboarding, campaign

execution, and reporting. Clearly outline the steps, responsibilities, and tools required for each process.

2. **Adopt Project Management Tools:**
   - Implement project management software to streamline task assignments, collaboration, and tracking. This will help your team stay organized and ensure projects are completed on time and within budget.

3. **Automate Repetitive Tasks:**
   - Identify repetitive tasks that can be automated to save time and free up resources. Use automation tools to streamline processes like content scheduling, social media posting, and reporting.

4. **Set Key Performance Indicators (KPIs):**
   - Define measurable KPIs for each department and role to track individual and team performance. Regularly review these KPIs to identify areas for improvement and recognize achievements.

5. **Foster Communication and Collaboration:**
   - Establish channels for effective communication and collaboration within your team. Encourage

regular meetings, brainstorming sessions, and knowledge-sharing to foster teamwork and innovation.

Developing a Culture of Collaboration, Innovation, and Continuous Learning

Creating a positive and collaborative work culture is vital for team growth and development. Here are some strategies to nurture such a culture:

1. **Encourage Knowledge Sharing:**
   - Create a supportive environment where team members are encouraged to share their knowledge, skills, and ideas. Host regular training sessions, workshops, or webinars to keep them updated with the latest trends and technologies.
2. **Promote Innovation and Creativity:**
   - Encourage your team to think outside the box and come up with innovative solutions to client challenges. Implement brainstorming sessions or ideation contests to stimulate

creativity and foster a culture of innovation.

3. **Recognize and Reward Excellence:**
    - Celebrate the achievements and milestones of your team members. Recognize their contributions and provide incentives or rewards to motivate them to excel in their roles.

4. **Provide Growth Opportunities:**
    - Offer opportunities for career growth and advancement within your agency. Provide mentorship programs, performance-based promotions, and cross-training opportunities to help your team members develop their skills and reach their full potential.

5. **Foster Work-Life Balance:**
    - Promote work-life balance and create a positive work environment. Encourage flexible working hours, provide necessary tools for remote work, and prioritize employee well-being.

By scaling your agency and growing your team, you will be able to handle more clients, expand your service offerings, and achieve sustainable growth. Hiring the right talent, establishing efficient processes, and fostering a culture of collaboration and continuous learning will ensure your agency's success in the dynamic digital marketing industry.

Next Steps

In the next chapter, we will explore the importance of diversifying your agency's services and revenue streams to meet evolving client needs and maximize profitability.

Chapter 8: Diversifying Your Agency's Services and Revenue Streams

In today's fast-paced digital marketing world, it's crucial for agencies to stay ahead by diversifying their services and revenue streams. By expanding what your agency offers, exploring new revenue opportunities, and developing strategic partnerships, you can enhance your capabilities and attract a broader range of clients. Let's dive into how you can achieve this.

Expanding Your Agency's Service Offerings

One effective way to diversify your agency's services is by expanding the range of digital marketing services you offer. As client needs and preferences evolve, it's essential to keep up with the latest trends and technologies. Broadening your service offerings can attract new clients and boost your revenue streams.

Start by conducting thorough market research to identify emerging needs and demands within the digital marketing industry. Keep an eye on new trends, technologies, and strategies that are gaining popularity. For instance, you might consider adding services such as influencer marketing, chatbot development, or video production to meet your clients' evolving needs.

Take a closer look at your current client base and identify any gaps in the services you provide. Are there areas where your clients are seeking assistance, but you currently don't offer those services? By expanding your offerings to fill these gaps, you can retain existing clients and attract new ones.

Exploring Additional Revenue Streams

In addition to expanding your services, it's beneficial to explore additional revenue streams that complement your agency's core offerings. This approach can create stability and resilience in your financial model.

Consider offering consulting services to clients who may not need full-scale digital marketing campaigns but could benefit from your expertise. Consulting can involve providing strategic advice, conducting audits, or offering training workshops to help clients improve their digital marketing efforts.

Another option is to offer white-label services, where you provide your expertise and services to other agencies under their brand name. This allows you to leverage your skills and resources to generate additional income without needing to acquire new clients independently.

Hosting training workshops and webinars can also be a lucrative revenue stream. Share your knowledge and expertise with other professionals in the industry who are looking to upskill or learn about specific digital marketing topics.

Lastly, consider exploring partnerships and collaborations with complementary businesses. This can include collaborating with web developers, graphic designers, or PR agencies to offer comprehensive marketing solutions to clients. By combining forces, you can leverage each other's strengths and tap into new client networks.

Developing Strategic Partnerships and Collaborations

Strategic partnerships and collaborations are vital for diversifying your agency's offerings and expanding your reach. Look for opportunities to align with other businesses that share a similar target audience or complement your services.

When exploring potential partnerships, consider the following factors:

1. **Complementary Services:** Identify businesses that offer services aligning with or enhancing your own. For example, if your agency specializes in SEO, consider partnering with a web development agency.
2. **Shared Target Audience:** Look for businesses that cater to a similar target audience. By partnering with them, you can tap into their client base and offer a more comprehensive range of services.
3. **Similar Values and Culture:** Choose partners that share similar values and work ethics. This will help ensure a smooth and compatible working relationship.
4. **Clear Communication and Collaboration Processes:** Define clear communication and collaboration processes to ensure efficient and effective collaboration with your partners.

Collaborating with other agencies or businesses can help you expand your service offerings without extensive investments in resources or talent. It also allows you to provide more comprehensive solutions to your clients, positioning your agency as a one-stop shop for all their digital marketing needs.

Conclusion

Diversifying your agency's services and revenue streams is key to staying competitive in the digital marketing industry. By expanding your service offerings, exploring additional revenue streams, and leveraging strategic partnerships, you can attract a broader range of clients, increase profitability, and position your agency for long-term success. Stay agile and adapt to the changing needs and demands of the digital landscape, ensuring that your agency remains relevant and valuable to clients.

Chapter 9: Managing Finances, Budgets, and Profitability

Managing finances, budgets, and profitability is crucial for the success and growth of your digital marketing agency. In this chapter, let's delve into the steps necessary to effectively manage your agency's finances and ensure its long-term profitability.

Setting Financial Goals and Budgets

When you start a digital marketing agency, setting clear financial goals and budgets is essential. These goals and budgets will guide your agency's operations, marketing initiatives, and growth strategies. Here's a step-by-step approach to help you set and manage your financial goals and budgets:

1. **Identify Your Financial Goals:**
   Begin by determining what you want to achieve financially. Whether it's reaching a specific revenue target, increasing profitability, or expanding your service offerings, having clear goals will provide direction.

2. **Conduct a Thorough Analysis:** Assess your agency's current financial situation, including revenue, expenses, and cash flow. Evaluating your past financial performance can help you identify areas for improvement or opportunities for growth.
3. **Set Realistic Budgets:** Based on your financial goals and analysis, develop budgets for different areas of your agency's operations, marketing, and growth initiatives. This will help you allocate resources efficiently and effectively.
4. **Monitor and Measure Progress:** Regularly track your agency's financial performance against your goals and budgets. This will enable you to identify any deviations early on and make necessary adjustments.
5. **Review and Revise:** As your agency grows and evolves, it's important to review and revise your financial goals and budgets. Adjust them accordingly to reflect the changing needs of your agency and the industry.

Implementing Financial Management Systems and Processes

To manage your agency's finances effectively, it's crucial to implement financial management systems and processes. These systems and processes will help you track expenses, revenue, and profitability accurately. Here are some steps to consider:

1. **Accounting Software:** Invest in reliable accounting software that suits your agency's needs. This will streamline financial record-keeping, invoicing, and financial reporting.
2. **Expense Tracking:** Implement a system for tracking all expenses, including salaries, office rent, software subscriptions, marketing expenses, and other overhead costs. This will help you understand where your money is going and identify areas where you can reduce expenses or reallocate resources.
3. **Invoicing and Billing:** Develop a clear and consistent invoicing and billing process to ensure timely payment by your clients. Use online invoicing tools or software to automate this process and reduce manual errors.

4. **Revenue Tracking:** Track your agency's revenue accurately by recording all payments received from clients. Categorize your revenue streams to gain insights into your most profitable services or clients.
5. **Profitability Analysis:** Regularly analyze your agency's profitability by comparing your revenue with your expenses. Identify areas where you can improve profitability, such as reducing costs or increasing prices for certain services.

Making Informed Decisions about Pricing, Billing, and Resource Allocation

Pricing your services, managing billing processes, and allocating resources effectively are vital aspects of managing your agency's finances. Here are some strategies to help you make informed decisions in these areas:

1. **Pricing Strategy:** Conduct market research and analysis to determine competitive pricing for your digital marketing services. Consider factors such as your agency's expertise, the value you provide to clients, and industry standards. Avoid underpricing

your services, as this can negatively impact your profitability.
2. **Billing Terms:** Clearly define and communicate your billing terms to clients. This includes payment due dates, late payment penalties, and any payment milestones or installments. Implement a system for tracking and following up on overdue payments.
3. **Resource Allocation:** Allocate your resources, such as time, manpower, and technology, effectively to maximize profitability. Regularly assess your agency's workload and client projects to ensure proper resource allocation and avoid overworking your team.
4. **Reinvestment and Growth:** Plan for reinvestment in your agency's growth. Allocate a portion of your profits for marketing initiatives, professional development, and upgrading your agency's infrastructure. This will help you stay competitive in the ever-evolving digital marketing landscape.

By effectively managing your agency's finances, setting clear financial goals, implementing financial management systems and processes, and making informed decisions about pricing, billing, and resource allocation, you can optimize profitability and ensure the long-term success of your digital marketing agency.

Chapter 10: Continuously Innovating and Adapting in the Digital Marketing Landscape

In the ever-changing world of digital marketing, keeping up with industry trends, emerging technologies, and best practices is crucial for your agency's success. By continuously innovating and adapting your strategies, services, and offerings, you can stay ahead of the competition and deliver exceptional value to your clients. This chapter will delve into the importance of staying up-to-date, investing in ongoing education and training, and the benefits of innovation and adaptation.

Staying Informed about Industry Trends and Emerging Technologies

The digital marketing landscape is constantly evolving, with new trends and technologies emerging regularly. It's essential for your agency to stay informed about these changes to remain competitive and provide cutting-edge solutions to your clients. Here are some ways to stay informed:

1. **Industry Publications and Blogs:**

- Subscribe to industry publications, blogs, and newsletters to stay updated on the latest trends, news, and insights in digital marketing. These resources often provide valuable information on emerging technologies, best practices, and case studies.
2. **Attend Conferences and Events:**
    - Participate in digital marketing conferences, workshops, and networking events. These gatherings bring together industry experts and thought leaders who share their knowledge and expertise. Networking with professionals in the field can also provide valuable insights and partnerships.
3. **Join Professional Associations and Communities:**
    - Join professional associations and online communities related to digital marketing. Engaging with other professionals in the industry can help you stay up-to-date with new trends, share knowledge, and collaborate on projects.
4. **Follow Influencers and Thought Leaders:**
    - Identify influencers and thought leaders in the digital marketing industry and follow them on

social media platforms. They often share valuable insights, opinions, and predictions. Engaging with their content can provide you with fresh perspectives and spark innovative ideas.
5. **Monitor Competitors:**
    - Keep an eye on your competitors to understand their strategies, service offerings, and innovations. Analyze their successes and failures to identify opportunities for improvement and differentiation.

Investing in Ongoing Education and Training

To stay at the forefront of the digital marketing industry, investing in ongoing education and training for yourself and your team is essential. Continuous learning keeps you updated with the latest tools, strategies, and techniques, enabling you to deliver high-quality services to your clients. Here are some ways to invest in education and training:

1. **Online Courses and Certifications:**
    - Enroll in online courses and certifications offered by reputable

institutions or platforms. These courses cover a wide range of digital marketing topics, such as SEO, PPC advertising, social media marketing, and content marketing. Completing these courses will enhance your skills and demonstrate your expertise to clients.

2. **Workshops and Webinars:**
   - Attend workshops and webinars conducted by industry experts. These events provide hands-on learning experiences and cover specific topics in depth. They are a great way to learn new skills and stay updated with the latest trends.

3. **Internal Training Sessions:**
   - Organize internal training sessions within your agency to share knowledge and expertise among team members. Encourage team members to share their insights, best practices, and experiences to foster a culture of continuous learning.

4. **Mentorship and Coaching:**
   - Seek mentorship and coaching from experienced professionals in the digital marketing industry. Their guidance and advice can

help you navigate challenges, provide new perspectives, and accelerate your professional growth.

Innovating and Adapting Your Agency's Strategies, Services, and Offerings

Innovation and adaptation are essential to not only survive but thrive in the digital marketing landscape. By continually evaluating and enhancing your agency's strategies, services, and offerings, you can deliver exceptional value to your clients and stay ahead of the competition. Here are some strategies for innovation and adaptation:

1. **Client Feedback and Insights:**
    - Regularly seek feedback from your clients to understand their evolving needs, pain points, and expectations. Use this feedback to improve your services, develop new offerings, and innovate your strategies.
2. **Experimentation and Testing:**
    - Embrace a culture of experimentation and testing within your agency. Test new tactics, platforms, and ideas to

identify what works best for your clients and stay ahead of industry trends.
3. **Embrace Emerging Technologies:**
    - Stay updated on emerging technologies, such as artificial intelligence, virtual reality, and voice search. Explore how these technologies can be integrated into your agency's services to enhance results and deliver innovative solutions to your clients.
4. **Collaboration and Partnerships:**
    - Foster collaborations and partnerships with other agencies, freelancers, or technology providers. These collaborations can help you extend your service offerings, access new markets, and leverage complementary expertise.
5. **Continuous Improvement:**
    - Regularly review and analyze the performance of your agency's strategies, services, and offerings. Identify areas for improvement and adapt accordingly. By continuously refining your processes and delivering exceptional results, you can build trust and loyalty with your clients.

Conclusion

In conclusion, staying informed about industry trends, investing in ongoing education and training, and continually innovating and adapting your agency's strategies, services, and offerings are crucial for success in the digital marketing landscape. By embracing these practices, you can position your agency as a leader in the industry, deliver exceptional value to your clients, and stay ahead of the competition.

www.ingramcontent.com/pod-product-compliance
Lightning Source LLC
Chambersburg PA
CBHW071221240526
45470CB00018B/2085